among sinners and saints

among sinners and saints

poems by
aileen bassis

SHANTI ARTS PUBLISHING

BRUNSWICK, MAINE

among sinners and saints

Published by Shanti Arts Publishing

Interior and cover design by Shanti Arts Designs

Shanti Arts LLC
193 Hillside Road
Brunswick, Maine 04011

shantiarts.com

Cover image— Arthimedes (AI) / AdobeStock
/ 574643030 / stock.adobe.com

Printed in the United States of America

ISBN: 978-1-962082-89-1 (softcover)

Dedicated to my father, Bouris Bassis.
His greatest gift to me was his deep love of the arts.

Contents

Acknowlegements 9

Gift for Apollo 13
A Photo from the 1930s 14
Poet 15
Among Sinners and Saints 16
On and Off the Dixie Freeway 18
Drawing Home 20
Mineral to Marrow 22
This Is Not Our World 23
Embody 24
Violence Lurks 25
Yet Another Bombing 26
Breath 27
Questions for America 28
In the Land of Second Chances 30
He Walks Away from Me 31
Too Many Stories Like This 32
Reading on Instagram 33
Imagine Flaubert 34
Matinee 35
Beckett and Buffet 36
Buzz 37
Waterkoude 38
Celluloid Flicker 40
Love Is Not a Myth in Chen's Garden Cafe 42
Early in December 43
Visitation 44
Time of the Dog 46
Forsaken City 48
The Last Time I Saw Karina 49
Viral Hours 50
Journey Back 51
Was ist Liebe 52
Disquietude 54
Not Knowing 55

Physics, the Body (and Marriage) 56

Doppelganger 57

Wait for Baby Girl 58

The Sun I Can't See 59

In Casaprota 60

Białowieza Forest 61

Between Lexicon and Road-Map 62

Some Say 63

This Was a Year When 64

A Physicist on the Radio 65

Eclipse 66

Acknowlegements

The author extends her gratitude to the editors of the following publications in which these poems previously appeared, sometimes in earlier versions:

Advice for Travelers (chapbook): "The Last Time I Saw Karina"

Amoskeag, The Journal of Southern New Hampshire University: "A Physicist on the Radio" (titled "Time Travels")

Cease Cows: "Breath"

Escape Wheel (anthology): "The Last Time I Saw Karina"

Glass, A Journal of Poetry: Poets Resist: "On and Off the Dixie Freeway"

Gravel Magazine: "Poet"

Great Weather for Media Poem of the Week: "In The Land of Second Chances"

Grey Sparrow Journal: "The Sun I Can't See"

JMWW: "In Casaprota" and "Visitation"

Leveler: "Mineral to Marrow"

Linden Avenue Literary Journal: "Wait for Baby Girl"

Newtown Literary: "Journey Back" and *"Waterkoude"*

The Other Side of the Mirror (chapbook): "Breath"; "Mineral to Marrow"; and "Questions for America"

Panoplyzine: "Reading on Instagram" (titled "A Poet Reads on Instagram")

Prelude: "Gift for Apollo" and "Bialowieza Forest"

Portland Review: "Embody"

Ravensperch: "Love is Not a Myth in Chen's Garden Cafe"

Sho Poetry Journal: "Not Knowing"

Shot Glass Journal: "Disquietude"

Sanctuary, Darkhouse Books (anthology): "Drawing Home"

Third Wednesday: "Eclipse"

Two Hawks Quarterly: "Questions for America"

Washington Square Review: "This Was a Year When"

The author also extends her gratitude to Long Island City Artists (LIC-A) and the New York State Council on the Arts (NYSCA) for their support.

Two things are infinite: the universe and human stupidity; and I'm not sure about the universe. There are only two ways to live your life. One is as though nothing is a miracle. The other is as though everything is a miracle.

—Albert Einstein

Gift for Apollo

sculpture by Robert Rauschenberg

The oracle on Delos did not envision
this door hammered
shut.

A wheeled door, not a chariot, but
a door-thing chained to a bucket waiting
to be filled with earth and ashes.

Why give this gift to Apollo?
A god, who longed for love
like you, like me.

Loved a boy
transformed into a flower,
loved a girl who became

a laurel tree and loved
a woman who betrayed him
with another.

When love is lost
what gifts can comfort us?

Here is offered
a shoulder-wide splash
of peach that's not skin,

blue that's not water, not sky,
but perhaps the violet-blue
of hyacinths, their petals smooth
as fingers tapping on your spine.

A Photo from the 1930s

Taken somewhere
in the Midwest.
A room at night.
A man lying in bed.

Did the photographer
knock or did he push
open an unlocked door?

Was the man asleep or did the door
creak and he turned away
hiding his face,
revealing only a pillowed oval
of hair and bare neck?

Or did he wake at a flashbulb's
pop and pull up the scalloped bedcover,
glance startled
into a camera's single eye
observing a girlie calendar on a wall,
his narrow bed, a bottle,
one cup on a chair beside him?

Did he push the sheet away,
scratch his chest, sit up to smoke
a Manila Blunt cigar, tasting
must and leather, feeling
mystery in the constant engine
of his heart—the puzzle
of his unmapped ramble
path along interstates and iron rails,
winding through halls
and stairs and all
the stops between.

Poet

Her hair
is a wheat
grass curtain, a blue
vein sprouts through
her chest to her
heart as words
drop like rocks
hitting the ground
then breaking to reveal
secret gleams of brown
and red, green
and even clean streaks
of milky quartz and some
words shoot out
like a cue ball looking to
make a ricochet
shot thunk to the corner
pocket and other
words
float
in the air, almost
unmoving, held
for a breath-beat
then land
like a fallen
bird that's not
ready to fly away.

Among Sinners and Saints

Walking through
    the museum
        past paintings
            doves and flames
            lilies and veils—
            a saintly martyr smiles.
                His body sprouts
                arrows—feathers
                   dazzle
                    gold, crimson, lapis blue
      —his feet touch earth but his head
      reaches to heaven   tiny angels
            dance all around.

        I study a grimacing metal face on a pedestal.
        The title reads "A Hypocrite
            and a Sinner." I can't tell if he's laughing or
                            screaming.

      Another room has photos of city streets.
      One frames a man in a crosswalk. His hand holds
      a cigarette — feathers of smoke   rise
      past his shoulder. His white shirt glows whiter
      than   a   ghostly   thumbprint
      of sun.   Not a saint — perhaps a sinner?

Outside the museum, fountains spurt—sprinkling water.
My feet hurt. Pigeons rise in a flurry. Smell of hotdogs.
A vendor has Trump items for sale and I avoid her eyes
as if she has a disease that I could catch. I try not to see
the legless beggar and a man asleep on a cardboard slab.

A woman walks   through the subway
car murmuring *chocolate*   with a tray
of bright candy for sale. Her baby rides
in a sling on her back sleeping   through
the subway noise.   His eyes open
and I see myself as two tiny slivers

floating
in his liquid gaze.
                   He doesn't
                        make a
                            sound.

On and Off the Dixie Freeway

In Florida motels are named for dreams of escape or hope
          or afterlife. There's Blue Lagoon

& Shangri-La & even Paradise Motel.
          Florida bears gifts of small surprises: a lizard

flicking an orange dewlap like a heart beating
          outside its body & a passing snake delivers

an atavistic shiver down my back & it's fun
          to drive around in my rented Chevy Cruze

on the North Dixie Freeway
          where a guy on a motorcycle passes me,

no helmet, ponytail in the wind, belly
          comfortably roosting on his legs like an old

song that keeps running in my head & I see
          a Confederate flag fluttering

from the back of his seat. I shouldn't be surprised,
          we're in Florida & this is the Dixie

Freeway, juddering through towns with statues
          of Stonewall Jackson & Robert E. Lee

with a history that fits me like someone else's
          clothes & when I reach my destination, waiting

for a show to start, hear a blonde lady say, *you
          can't sit there*

to the singer with dark skin & twisted locs
          & the singer answers, *this chair is mine, I'll sit*

where I want & everyone keeps chatting & I sip
      white wine & nibble snacks

while mosquitoes keen around my head & I don't
      know what to scratch.

Drawing Home

Four lines make a square
without a window or a door.
No way in and no way

out. Can you call this
home? Draw more. Two
lines meet and slant. A roof

perhaps. Do you remember
when you pressed your thumb
against a splinter

to mark that place
with blood, held a fistful
of dirt from your mother's

garden? Loud bursts
and air filled with wet
and flakes and flesh.

Have you smelled metal burning?

Ask me about the touch of insect
legs, the spiral screech of birds,
the wall's dripped color.

There was
a shore where water
peeled back like skin

and foam glimmered hunger.
Gulls were sharp needles pulling
white through a cloth sky.

Find a way back for me. Draw
a map, show me where
to turn right or left.

Draw a door, draw
windows. Look, pigeons
are flying. What vibrates inside
each body to guide them home again?

Mineral to Marrow

Vitrines of muskets, pikes.
Six knives, a stained wool coat.
A confederate flag.

> Portrait of the plantation owner
> in blue satin—imperious crooked arm,
> curled wig. Opaque gaze.

You can't read his expression
but move closer to find your reflection
makes you part of this puzzle.

> Mineral to marrow, we're roped
> together, beyond grace, in a knot
> that cuts too harsh for metaphor.

How did it feel to own another?
The other day, a cop in Georgia
said, we only kill black people.

This Is Not Our World

a book lies open to a picture
painted with a brush of squirrel hairs,
with colors: lead-white and indigo
and yellow named for naples

there's a man sleeping in a meadow
and a woman on a donkey
with hands folded around a stiff
swaddle of child who looks
out from the page with flat eyes

smaller than a grain of rice
with an oval mouth drawn precisely
as the wall of bricks stacked
amid blades of grass
dotted with madder-rose
and deeper crimson

around trees whose branches
arc beyond desire and sky
echoing into blue and more blue
inside this goldleaf frame
with not a shadow anywhere

all topped by a touch of sun
holding fast to a day that cannot
end in this world of all beginnings
where even time is dozing
in the meadow in the grass
that's forever green.

Embody

The New York Times, October 24, 2019
"LONDON—The 39 people found dead in a refrigerated
truck trailer in southeastern England . . . "

We don't know much. The authorities said they were
Chinese. Later, police said they were from a village in
Vietnam. Probably seeking work in factories or
construction or nail salons in Britain.

We don't know much but I can imagine: Polyester and
cotton shirts. Lipstick in a back pocket, a wallet,
creased photos, cigarettes. Long hair and short, bristles
trailing across a chin, blemished skin or smooth cheeks
curving to dip around silent open lips.

We don't know if one man told his wife that money
would arrive soon. Or if one woman thought about the
smell of her baby's hair or if anyone remembered
laughter spilling like water from a glass.

Violence Lurks

is it a feeling
that breathes in and out like a lover
in your ear or is does it draw

moments deep until a current
pulls you way past thought and you
don't care if you can ever make it back

to shore or let yourself be
pulled under or is it like licking
a body that's warm with waiting

until you can't dream another moment
as it drinks you up and leaves you dry
and thirsting for some more?

Yet Another Bombing

I can't
imagine dirt inside
your mouth
your nose
your eyes

I can't imagine
blasts echoed inside
your stomach—snaking
through your bowels
and groin and down your legs,

I can't imagine an oily curtain
of smoke rising from a black-lipped
pit while shouts
blare and careen

and the litter of road and rock
shards of metal and cloth
muscle
organs
bones
scatter
into careless dark.

Breath

first is breath (remember a doctor saying, "wait, don't push" and you floundering on waves roiling through your body, puffing in and out until "now," and you push and out slides a baby—purple tiny feet, a gray-white cord that the doctor moves from the baby's neck and you hear a cry and know the baby took a breath—life spread before you like a maze of roads streaming to a sea that is forever salt as the waters that filled your womb) think now of George's mother or Eric's or all the other mothers that waited for a child's breath until he's a man and then his breath is lost and you wonder how or what became of those tiny milk-teeth, rolled beneath a bed-frame, tossed upon the floor.

Questions for America

is that you america
in a hallway
or hurrying down subway stairs
or ambling through the dollar store
credit card in hand?

are you standing at a bus stop
or pulling up beside me at a stoplight
& driving off before the light
turns from red to green

& is this all yours america,
can you hold it in your hands?
towers & strip-malls
shingles & vinyl siding & garbage mounds
black as crows pecking at the bags

—& how about the sky
america & rivers hemmed
with bridges & shores
split by railroad tracks
& I wonder how you're feeling
america—if your head hums
if your belly's empty
if you need a drink
a nibble
a man-sized meal?

—taste me america
my salty sweat
my sweet perfume
my sticky crumbs

will you break me
with a snap like knuckles cracking
or whisper sleep tight & pull
the covers up? because I wonder
if you dream of me & maybe
you're wandering
in a tunnel cold as doubt's

fingers resting on your neck
& you can't see a beginning
or know which way to go

so tell me if you're still breathing
america
let me hold a mirror to your lips

In the Land of Second Chances

you always have an umbrella
and the ATM says your account
has lots of money—do you want
that cash in twenties or fifty
dollar bills? and in the land
of second chances, black teens
stroll through a mall and stores
don't lock the doors and black
men lope through suburbs and no
one calls the cops and in the land
that isn't here and in a time
that isn't now, police don't
shove black bodies
to the ground and bones won't
break and blood won't stain sidewalks
but stay where it belongs, pumping
into each heart and arteries and veins.

In the land of second chances
air swoops into lungs
and out and in again
in a beat as constant as day
falling into night and morning
light strokes a hand across
each face and lips
move with words
that almost sound
like song.

He Walks Away from Me

I said—Don't
walk away
Remember that story about dying
that said our spirits will cross a river
On a raft to reach another life
Don't walk away
If you jump off that raft into lightless
water—will you sink?
Will you drink cold river—or thrash arms—kick hard
until you reach
a shore or a rock
where you could pull
Yourself up out of the black? and then—will you be caught
between life here and some-
where else?

Walking under white-bright sun—Listen—Life's

a wild animal
that will eat
your heart—Don't

walk away
where
will you go?
Nowhere is everywhere

Too Many Stories Like This

She posted, "he's the man I love."

It's a thin
wavering
line along love
and the line
separating kisses
from bites
and the lines from
fingers pinched around a nipple
to fingers squeezed around a throat
and lines smudged
by mascara running
wet with tears
of anger or tears
from pain but
nobody laughs or even smiles
when the line gets crossed
by a stroke across
a cheek that turns
into a slap
against
a body grasping blood,
piss, sweat,
and then
a brain
gone blank,
eyes shut, mouth
slack.

One
punch and she hit a wall
and fell.

Then he
dragged her
out.

Reading on Instagram

first is voice/ its raspy-edged buzz/ rough
enough to catch in a throat or scratch out
a pause/ a glottal intake as if words would
be taste/ licked like a spoon/ drips tapping
like a faucet left slightly open in another
room/ like a wind-up watch turning
minutes inside and out

or wait now/ if that's first/   then next is
thought rising/   heady as cut lawns or
fresh asphalt cooling   or a hot wave
beckoning from an open grate/ edgeless
as water that comes and goes and returns
weed-strewn and filled with gifts of tiny
shells and pebbles rubbed smoother than
a sound

Imagine Flaubert

waking damp, entangled
in his bed.

Imagine Emma holding
her lover's letter up
to the light. Inked words
flutter, alive as insects.

He brushed his finger
along a framed portrait
of Louise, sees dust rise.

Emma's mind is a polished chest
of drawers
opening and closing, some bare
wood, empty
as a mouth and others
ripe with silk.

Bright morning sun.
He squints, tugs a curtain
across the window, pulls
a loose thread near the hem.
A row of tiny holes
glint pins of light
and he recalls pleated sleeves
dropping from her shoulders,
her mouse-soft slipper on the floor.

Beeswax
rubbed into wood shines
desire into thought.

He wrote to Louise: *others may feel
nothing but contempt after possession,
but I am not like them, and I glory
in not being so. On the contrary, for
me possession breeds
affection.*

She remembers
Rodolphe's room,
his bed,
his sweat.
How she washed between her legs.

Matinee

Bell ringing. Darkness, then light like pink frosting skims an actor walking centerstage. A skitter of violins crinkle notes. Rows of faces tilt up—hopeful as goldfish in a bowl waiting for a treat. Trumpets waver into their denouement as actors link hands, flat against a shadowed set. Arms sweep as a plum velvet wall descends and houselights brighten catching flecks of dust spiraling down. Actors take their final bows, shake off their fictions.

A snoring man wakes, clutches his phone, "The weather, what's it doing out?" Programs scatter. Scarves, hats, gloves. Noses are blown. Outside the open doors, wheels push gray slush. Huge flakes of snow are falling. Cold fingers on buttons. The crush of wool against your cheek. How did the story begin?

The subway entrance yawns its indifference, a fumbled farecard, thoughts of groceries, phone vibrating in your pocket. The pastiche of columns and gilded trees, chorus and arias, the brass glissando, dissolving like sugar stirred into tea.

Beckett and Buffet

"What do I know of man's destiny?
I could tell you more about radishes."
   —Samuel Beckett

A stage set without motion or is it
motive? Brick walls, shuttered windows
and is a body hulking under a dirty cloth?
This is a blind man's game after all.
We shrink under a litany of words
but afterwards we dine and drink
at the All You Can Eat Buffet.

Like the Irish seer who spoke of destiny
over a plate of radishes, we survey
warming trays arrayed before us
at Skyline Cafe on Fairview Ave.

The steam table exhales an open mouth
of hot mist and above the trays a vista blurs
asphalt and power lines into a smear
of sand and muck. Random as pick-up
sticks, concrete barriers scatter on blacktop.

Cracked shell of earth. Swamp grass
stutters its revelation—the triumph
of feral cats.

Failed king, lost queen, our game
may be over. Should we rise
to clap? Ask for more? Remember
your hat before you go.

Buzz

smell—marijuana oily pungent
mist coiling out of doorways
to sidewalks that sprout sun-licked

girls gleaming sharp light
cheeks flowering into red
hot-fleshed babies dangle feet

soft as cupcakes dotted with
pale candy as tables fill
with fried potatoes piled

on paper plates spreading grease
growing translucent with zig-zags
of ketchup

in an irresistible ooze
as sky shifts blue deeper
than puddles of blue lemonade

sand finding its way
between toes as dust-sprinkled
wind skates over concrete gravel

crossing a stubbled not-lawn but
a plastic green illusion—air
tickling purple globes of allium

engulfed by ceaseless clouds of bees
buzzing tribute to each
tiny tiny summer bloom.

Waterkoude

i read today
the Dutch have a word,   *waterkoude*
                             it's damp
                             it's cold

waterkoude
wraps around your bones

i read
i walk   i walk by the river

a woman's rising from a bench by a wall
                i walk

        a woman rises from a bench

                        her body
                        echoes ancient caryatids   like stone
                                                       made flesh
            she bears the weight of day   her thick arm twists
                        hair in a coil against her neck

                    i walk   i walk

she lifts her phone to a cheek that
                could entice
                    a god
to return to mortal life   she asks "*cuando,*
cuando mi amor"
                i walk

white sky above us all
                    one hawk
                    rides the air
                    sweet as water that never knew a tide

it's damp   it's cold
        waterkoude
what word   what words
can words bind this moment

                it slips
                a soft   soft-fingered thief
                            twisting a lock   i hear
                            tumblers click
                i walk
        i read a word

                        waterkoude

Celluloid Flicker

Doves are cooing and fields of grapevines
should be idyllic but there's the smell

of manure everywhere. A Citroen
stops—a woman runs out.

She looks familiar; I almost
call out a name, but I don't

know her, after all—I'm in France.
A man walks by with shirtsleeves

rolled up to display his biceps, a cigarette
stub leans from his lips

reminding me of Jean-Paul Belmondo
and I'm surprised to remember the word

lèvres—I didn't think I learned
anything in high school French.

Swallows swoop above
in a cold wind that has a name

that escapes me and bird cries
meld with church bells and like

a window shutter blowing open,
a vision appears of Jean Seberg

standing on a bed and Belmondo,
slouched below eyeing her legs

that are smooth as the marble
body I saw the day before

—Aphrodite in her controposto stance
beside the remains of a Roman ship

—a scrambled cluster of broken timbers
like my thoughts melting

with the taste of madeleines
on my tongue.

Love Is Not a Myth in Chen's Garden Cafe

they were young/ the dark-haired dark-eyed girl/ her tiny skirt climbing her laddered tights revealing a patchwork of pale olive and across from her was a boy or maybe he was a young man/ maybe he had already left boyhood behind/ he was explaining everything to her/ how to hold her chopsticks/ the surprises of dim sum/ how you don't know what's inside but it all will be delicious/ and she/ and she was all beauty with a spill of hair dancing each time she raised her chin and did i say that they were young? and he was talking talking talking with one leg vibrating from his hip down to his untied sneaker beating against a tiled floor/ there was hot tea that smelled of flowers and he asked do you like spicy? a waiter with hair tipped in a yellow halo shuffled in and out from a hot kitchen where a paunchy cook hovered in a cloud of steam to send forth his offering/ a special platter of pork belly and bright hot peppers glistening like a prayer and she pressed chopsticks to a strand of meat, swallowed and said it's really good/ and will they bring us rice? he said yes, yes they always bring rice but did i tell you, did i say/ that she was beauty incarnate and who wants who needs a god or any prayers when you're so very young and your bowl is always filled with rice.

Early in December

after moths have given
    up their doomed flitter to the lamp
        before winter presses against the window
and enters through cracks along the sill
    before evening clicks shut
        with the heft of a metal door
fitting into the jamb
    when the clock flashes numbers
        ascending and descending in a path
inevitable as the fridge tumbling ice cubes into a freezer's
    plastic box and before
        we waken dust grains from our
stacks of books and before your arm
    lies heavy across my thigh
        we search for a song
whose name we've both forgotten
    and yet its music enters tender
        as cat's paws to nestle
between us and pour a glimmer
    violet as satin
        and certain as your body
warm against my own

Visitation

Among spent tulips and empty coffee cups,
a pigeon lands beside me in the park.
He coos.

One bead of eye stares back
glimmering like a dropped coin
and when his beak opens
I almost think he's about to speak.

I remember reading a line from Rilke with you,
Perhaps the same bird echoed through both of us
yesterday, separate, in the evening.
    In the winter, you heated soup,
    we paged through your book
    of Italian paintings, marveling
    at rows of worshipers and saints,
    their humble feet.

Who else thinks of you?

You've been gone for many years.

Your eyes were like fractured marbles,
were they hazel or streaky green?

I remember the faint brush of corduroy,
your cheekbone's thrust beneath your skin
and a moment when sun lit
the bristly edges of your hair
into a halo
and I recall our last phone call.
Your voice was strange
as if you were in a land
of static and dropped connections.

If only you could return
in purple-gray feathers
to tell me of roosting in treetops,
of puddles' cool caress,
of your dominion over sparrows
and disdain for heavy creatures
who can't lift wings and fly.

But light as floating pollen,
hollow as a bird-bone,
once more you slip away.

Time of the Dog

I heard
whining
behind me.
I turned. A dog
was following me.
He gripped
my shoelaces,
began to chew. I opened
the door, before
I could stop him, he dashed
in, jumped up
onto the sofa, raised
a russet leg and began
to gnaw.

He seems larger
every day. My
apartment fills
with his smell.
His thin teeth test
the skin
around my wrist
as if he's wondering
how I'd taste.

At night, I wake
to his snore and wonder
if he's dreaming
of other times and places.
Perhaps he's bored.
Does he long
for a change of scene?
I scratch along
his backbone,
and tell him about
the Arizona desert,

of giant trees out
west, of paddles dipping
into cold rivers up north.
His eyes track shadows
across the ceiling.
His nose twitches
at the sounds
of a distant crash,
at shouts,
at cries.

Maybe
this is the morning
when he'll share
his animal secrets:
how to roll your
spine in grass,
how
to vibrate
your intentions
gently
behind
your teeth,
how to shape
the fathomless grip
of sinew under flesh.

Forsaken City

Dark rooms and shrouded terraces. Morning weighs air that's thick with longing. I envy the countless insects underfoot and their mindless scurry and I even envy the silence of pebbles on the street.

                              We are left
                           with shuttered
                                  stores
                                   trash
                        and tweedy shrubs

        A vacant bus runs north and south
        along the boulevard,

                    abandoned as a distant moon
                          or comet traveling
                                out of sight.

The Last Time I Saw Karina

music slips restless fingers into pockets of conversation as we listen
to Karina speak without a pause/ her pale-egg face crushed beneath
black hair streaming away like her kiss that missed my cheek/ I
recall a portrait I've seen many times by the painter Soutine/
a woman in red/ coat sliced open/ fingers meeting in a nervous
steeple/ not really listening/ I imagine Soutine's village in Europe's
east before the war/ shrouded in birches/ peat smoke everywhere/
each night plowed into another day/ life chewed like black bread
until Soutine was lost in the Holocaust/ and through our
entrees and dessert/ Karina tangles streets in cities she's never
seen/ grandmother's house in Warsaw/ a shop in Toulouse/
the embassy in Lisbon where her father waited for visas
to escape/ she mixes stories with her list of ailments/ stomach
troubles/ fitful nights/ foggy thoughts/ she can't remember the
number on the house in France/ and were ten cousins lost or
twelve/ and where did her mother's sisters go/ she sips some
wine/ declares she shouldn't drink with all her meds/ grabs
her husband's cane to walk to the ladies room/ limping/ first
with her right leg/ then dragging her left/ turns back to tell
us that gluten makes her ill or maybe it's the new pills or
a virus without a name/ showers crumbs through this dining
maze of high-top stools and stony tables/ I hear the music
change to a wail with a pounding beat/ I'm tired/ I want
to go and beckon to the waiter/ he extends an arm tattooed
with a scroll of dripping daggers/ his lips part/ white teeth
gleam and he bows before us like a supplicant without a
prayer to ask/ what else can he bring? was everything all right?

Viral Hours

A key rattles—sounds thrum
inside walls, waver through the airshaft.

Is someone in the hall? Four
o'clock tastes flat as three.

Each minute dissolves into the next.
You long to sharpen your

mind to a point, precise
as a needle. Lick

a thread and pull. Atoms stitch
futures spinning slow and slower

and closer yet. Here's the remote.
Click to the last screen. A chyron runs

below groomed heads. An aquarium
of fluid lips on mute, they swim,

pixelate, transform. Random as thought,
they possess your afternoon.

Journey Back

hurtling through tunnels
across islands under rivers
we sway
weary as the salt-washed warrior
who wandered the seas for years
our fingers tapping as screens flicker
newsfeed hums
posting battles won & battles
lost   phones tumble songs
          a child's voice seeps out
words folding into tiny packages like origami
          elephants & peacocks

we're here & yet not
sounds recede & rise
          brief sails against a line of water

          the greeks called the horizon
          "the bounding circle" & we're
held in that curve between our world & what's above

          glass blackens
          then flashes & we travel
                    from dark to dazzle
                    past the expectancy of doorways

to a hall that narrows round
a mirror's steady eye & you wonder
what's there in that dusky
passage

where a door sighs open
to a room   familiar & strange
          as your reflection
where a half-blind dog shifts
a heavy body & leans against your thigh

Was ist Liebe

"What's Love" (German)

i was nineteen when i dropped
out of college
went to california
where i looked
for a job and pined after
a shy-eyed brown-haired boy
with a lilting way of moving
like tall reed grass bending on
dry berkeley hillsides
and an older guy
with a wide red face
and a failed marriage
clinging to the back
of his neck asked me
to go see tina turner
and i said sure i love
her big wheel turning song
and those legs flashing
from her fringed dress but i
didn't want to have sex
with him
so i didn't go see tina
and four or five years
later i was back in new york
filled with questions about what
i wanted or what kind
of person i might become
or what i wanted to say
or if i had anything
to say and questions
kept running like
a movie soundtrack
that's out of sync
so words come on
too soon or too late

and you kinda know
what's happening but
nothing's smooth
and nowhere's easy
and i wasn't sure
of anything
or anyone and you said hey
tina turner is playing the felt
forum and your eyes
were watchful
steady-green
and i started
to think this might
be something
more
but i hadn't thought
of those years in a while
until last week when
the news was full
of stories about tina
passing and how she
learned german and her
husband
gave her his kidney
and i recalled
our night at the garden
seeing tina sing
and dance and now
i don't have
any questions left
about what's
love.

Disquietude

Each day takes another bite
of certainty melting into a
puddle clinging to the bottom
of each hour—but you're no good
at figuring out the odds—there may be cause
& effect but does the checkbook
ever need to balance? traffic
never stops & a faithless
river teems with boats & barges
& flagrant jet skis bouncing
with abandon/ maybe all you need
is a drink/ crack open the fridge
to the wanton call of
soda & some cheese/ a regretful
olive
rolling on a plate

—you thought
at least you have

your body but
that grows into a stranger
too.

Wait, I'm asking
someone, anyone

please, pull
down the shades—let's keep

it dark/ an open faucet is spilling
curses

& as for me, I'm waiting
for quiet
to stretch across my sheet.

Not Knowing

remember the winter
when we were living in that cold cold loft—we didn't know
how cold we would be on sundays when there was only enough
heat to keep the pipes from freezing and a single space heater
flickered red with a paltry groan of defeat as it warmed
nothing in the high-ceilinged open space wafting cat smells
and cooking oil from the topless bar below and
remember Miguel and Jane—their two children drinking
hot cups of cocoa gripped in small smooth hands
and how they looked at me with eyes
clear as unshattered glass and remember that night
—Miguel drunk—his shirt torn—his elbows
thrust through his ragged white sleeves—you threw him
out and locked the door—he stood raging and roaring
to Jane in the jaundice-lit street below—she said
don't let him in—he'll be okay tomorrow—then
she asked me—*do you want kids* and I didn't know
what to say—it was a thought as unreadable to me then
as an ancient language in a dusty book and I said no
—I thought motherhood would be like stepping into traffic
without a glance right or left and I didn't know
if anyone would stop or where to find
the faith or surety to help me get across

Physics, the Body (and Marriage)

Physicists pose theories: there's "spooky"
entanglement, a connection between particles
that continues despite separation and across distance.
Recently muon particles were discovered—
a new force of nature that doesn't follow rules,
"wobbly" puzzles to decipher like dark matter
filling a third of our universe
or dark energy pulling everything apart
but in the here and now
we're under siege from an unseen
virus floating through the air, mutating
into variations that nest inside our bodies
and invade my every thought.

One night my husband lay beside me in the throes
of illness. I thought of his mysteries:
of his skin and hair, fingernails and lips,
genitals and teeth and our puzzle
of married life with selves separate
and yet entangled, intimate
as muon particles passing through
our bodies and everything else
on our planet until they decay
in less time then it takes to kiss
good-night and turn
off our bedroom lamp.

Doppelganger

You may think
yourself
light
of a reflection
you find
and recognize
a shoulder
your own and you're
inside the body
but never see
us and never leave
the crowd parts
you feel
against
rooted
and you're rapt
a turning twist
to yesterday

you know
but in this
that's a reflection
in a mirrored doubling
yourself in a crowd
a gait a tilting chin
shrug like
wondering—are you dividing like cells
multiplying like universes you've heard of
like mysteries that swallow
a trace and when
for a moment
a body pressing
your body is familiar
deep as your bones
held by an unknowing slide
that may be an end
or is hinting of tomorrow

Wait for Baby Girl

seated at the window of Sweetleaf Coffee/ watching cars
go from the foot of the Pulaski Bridge to Brooklyn & back/
turning on Eleventh Street & onto 48th/ past brick & glass
& under trains skimming along an elevated track/ the #30 bus
sweeps around/ moves across Jackson with motorbikes/ bicycles/
strollers/ a pink-lipped woman with fuchsia gloves walks
by/ her hair is a red-brown tangle matching three dogs leashed
together in a triangle of fur & tongues bound to a man
trailing earbud wires & cigarette smoke/ I watch a woman
& a little girl/ in pink/ jacket/ hat & tights run to make the light

outside the window/ everything is motion while inside
Sweetleaf Coffee everything is still except the barista
at the counter throwing napkins in the trash & a music
mix playing ohbabybabybaby/ Christina tells me a baby
is growing in her belly/ she glows like a woman in my
book of medieval art/ a painted mother looking down
at her solemn baby who stares out from the picture
as if to say/ I'm here now/ what
happens next?

oh pinkpinkpink/ a girl is coming in the spring/ baby
baby/ what will be her name? I say maybe a flower
like Daisy or Violet but Christina doesn't answer/ she
closes her eyes & she's quiet as if listening to a seashell
pressed against her ear & she says wait mamá/ wait/
we'll meet her in the spring

The Sun I Can't See

"making a bit of pink"
—James Schuyler, "February"

Colors spill, as many as a crayon
box, all 72, blossoming bucolic:
trees, shrubs, tulips. Even
a baby turns pink
in rosy light.

      But maybe
that's somewhere
else or maybe
never was. This city rolls heavy,
raucously remaking,
revising; shoving grass into park
squares so leashed dogs can proudly
squat and defecate. Broken
whiskey bottle bits
wink beside rubbery leaves..

      This stormy May
battered weak trees. Stumps
and branches line the curbs.
Sidewalks scumble with everyone
flowing in choppy thought
eddies to anywhere
but here.

      Now, let's take a break
because June sky's
is exhaling peach and gold.

Press one button and spring
lifts its express elevator
to the penthouse floor
and *there*, a woman
stands and glows.

In Casaprota

Look darling, crocuses are blooming
at our feet with petals open like hands waiting
to receive our gifts. Has Autumn
taken a few days off
to ride away on the back of a Vespa,
arms melting round a man smelling
of hair gel, starch and lust?

O the sun is brighter than a taste of limoncello.
Someone's calling, *Bella, Bella Signora,*
from the crowd at Bar Micarelli but I can't see
who it is. Wind blurs my eyes—I grip your arm.
Hold me steady on this broken pavement.
But no, we've been misled—Autumn's here,
her slip winking below her skirt.

Thirsty dear? Want a spritz? Aperol or Campari?
WhatsApp is vibrating my phone back to life
with jpgs of toddlers smearing strawberries
across their cheeks. I'll take that as a sign to drink
Campari. The tumbler's red gleam is an omen
that only birds can read and I'll cry
ciao to everyone as we drive
over cobblestones and Peroni cans.
And just when I think this trip is over
a cat will meow, *Aspetta un momento,*
her mouth open as a seashell
her nose blooming into crocus pink.

Białowieza Forest

Let's lose ourselves in our city of stucco

and brick, in crowds swarming through cross-

walks and pooling over sidewalks. What's there

below the loose flap of scaffolds and lights

turning on and off? Will we walk once more

through damp-walled alleys in Venice,

hear water lapping at every turn, or stand

on a shore in Skagen where

the North Sea meets the Baltic

in a line of pulsing waves

that have no end, hear seals

barking beside rusting oil tankers

from the east. When will we

see that moss-thick Polish forest

of oak and pine, green shadows ribbed white

with birch? Don't ask for anything.

Great-horned aurochs have vanished

from that forest and soon, the wild bison

will be no more.

Between Lexicon and Road-Map

Misheard or misunderstand
      words crumpling into sound until sense
is dry—a leaf, a dead insect body,
a clipped nail and after all,
words are frail or inconsequential when compared
to this sea-swell of events floating on tides ruled
not by the moon but chatter that may be a diatribe
or perhaps a blessing. You mutter—almost
a prayer but for what? Surcease, surfeit, what
future waits for you? Mount this
slippery ride. Beast or machine?
It purrs—smells of heat, of wet
you feel teeth glow. You ask
what else—your tongue drips why.

Some Say

this world is getting us ready for the next or that
the past is elastic
stretching from this moment
into another

and when winter's arm leans
against your waist—a rough
hand catches
your cheek—throbs a hum
intimate as pain and familiar
as an uninvited guest
who drinks all your wine and never
wants to leave

This Was a Year When

anger seeded the earth
brushing past a moment's
craving for release while
       we found ourselves
driving dry-
eyed on a road without a sign
for where to get off or turn
       leaving us
grateful for light
hoping that the moon would
illuminate our night and longing for
joy in small phrases or a sound we
knew or wanted as erratic weather
lifted air into
motion then snapped dry
now—then left us
open-mouthed
praying with reshaped words to
quiet us or found like portents of
rolling clouds or nails
scratching your skin
trailing along your neck
unremembered moments
violent as night pulls down
       the shades as curtains blow open
       to an unknown body breathing
       out and in
we wished for night but not now
x-claiming
yet unforgiven—
zigzag away this, our bounded
       repentant year.

A Physicist on the Radio

was talking about time.
It never stays still,
not motionless like
craters on the airless moon
but crumbles and grows dusty,
time growing more disorganized
as cells lapse into forgetting
to stop or getting lost, appearing
days later like a single sock
trapped inside a clean sheet.

My mother traveled time
through the milky way
of dementia. Scrambled it, cutting
in days from seventy or eighty
years ago like creaming butter
sliced into sugar.

Mixed or poured, folded
front to back or side to side,
time floats without a recipe.
Moving out of reach between herds
of neurons and twitchy dendrites,
remote as quasars
and jittery as her brainwaves.

Eclipse

from Greek *ekleipsis*—a forsaking,
from *ekleipein*—to abandon,
from *leipein*—to leave

I don't know
the laws of the universe
or understand
the undulations of sound or how
a snake crossing my path
is at once
both beautiful and terrible.

I don't know what lies coiled inside us
invisible as a black hole
consuming stars
and I don't know if stars sense
they're being swallowed
as they're pulled like swimmers
caught in a riptide.

I don't know the chemistry that floats inside us
or what vibrates in your veins
to pierce the membrane around your cells
or where in the folded loops of your brain
is that afternoon one August
when we sat on lawn chairs
eyes behind cardboard glasses
watching a black moon
float across a still sun.

How birds grew silent
in the arms of gray trees
and shadows pooled over knee-deep weeds
and above us in that unlit unfolding
we saw a glimpse of returning sun
that held out a promise
imperfect as any other.

AILEEN BASSIS is a visual artist and poet in New York City with a practice in book arts, printmaking, photography, and installation. She is the author of two chapbooks: *The Other Side of the Mirror* (Unlikely Books) and *Advice for Travelers* (Black Sunflowers Press). She has been awarded two poetry residencies to the Atlantic Center for the Arts, a fellowship in poetry from the Yaddo Foundation, and grants in literature from NY State Council on the Arts as well as the Queens Arts Fund. Her poems appear in four anthologies and many journals including *The Pinch*, *Spillway*, *The Southampton Review*, *Canary*, and *Prelude*.

www.ingramcontent.com/pod-product-compliance
Lightning Source LLC
Chambersburg PA
CBHW022041090426
42741CB00007B/1149